T0014574

Philip L Evans

POWERFUL CONFESSIONS TO RENEW YOUR MIND

Based on eight revelations
of the character of God

WESTBOW
PRESS®
A DIVISION OF THOMAS NELSON
& ZONDERVAN

Scripture taken from the New King James Version®. Copyright © 1982 by Thomas Nelson. Used by permission. All rights reserved.

WestBow Press books may be ordered through booksellers or by contacting:

WestBow Press
A Division of Thomas Nelson & Zondervan
1663 Liberty Drive
Bloomington, IN 47403
www.westbowpress.com
1 (866) 928-1240

ISBN: 978-1-9736-4643-3 (sc)
ISBN: 978-1-9736-4644-0 (e)

Library of Congress Control Number: 2018913815

Print information available on the last page.

WestBow Press rev. date: 11/28/2018

My dear friend and colleague Philip Evans has written this excellent book which is needed for our generation more than ever.

I have known Philip for nearly 30 years and I want to say that he is one of the finest Bible teachers I have heard. He is extremely thorough in his teaching and leaves no stone unturned.

This book should be read by leaders as well as all believers who want to grow to maturity in all things.

I highly recommend this book and look forward to seeing many more from this mighty man of God!

Trevor Newport, International Coalition of
Apostolic Leaders.

This is a wonderful book written by a man who has made it his life practice. I have always loved the covenant names of God and this book has broken them down into wonderful understandable and accessible chunks. I encourage anyone who wants to know God and his power in their lives to read this and make confession their daily practice also. Their life will never be the same again.

God bless you Philip
Kingsley Armstrong, President, International Gospel
Outreach

We have known Philip and Margaret for 5 years and had the privilege of together leading a Love Wales Ministry School in North Wales. We know Philip as a man of great integrity and humility, who lives and ministers the truths in this book. He sees the miraculous and gives the glory to God. We are confident that this book will be a wonderful resource for all, grounded in the Word of God, and providing very Biblically based declarations. We know from experience the power of declarations based on the Word of God, and the intentional application of this book will be life changing!

Rev Geoff and Jane Blease, Living Stones Ministries, and Love Wales Team

INTRODUCTION

Various people have told me that I should write a book, and numerous ideas have passed through my mind at different times. At first, I thought that I should write about all the things I have seen in Nepal and other places on mission trips, but I had always struggled with finding the time and sometimes questioned my motives. So, although I have made a start on occasions, the whole idea was shelved until recently. Just a few months ago, I knew what I should write about, and the words flowed relatively easily, so here it is!

This book is about changing our thinking or renewing our minds, as the Bible describes it. The mind can be like a battlefield! It is where sin can be conceived or where creative ideas can be birthed. It is where anxiety and stress can get a grip or where the word of God can be processed and peace can be felt. The power and effect of what goes on in our minds cannot be over emphasized.

The message of this book has come out of the experience of life. Having struggled in so many areas, putting into practice the truths outlined in these pages has brought about a transformation, and although I know I am not what I will be, I also know that I am not what I used to be! The Bible says that we have the mind of Christ, but what does this mean and how do we make it real in our lives?

It is my prayer that everyone who reads this book will experience a transformation to become more like Christ. It is not intended to be an easy remedy for all problems but rather to be seen as part of the armor of God, given to every child of His and to be practiced on a daily basis.

ACKNOWLEDGEMENTS

I want to acknowledge all those (far too many to name) who, over many years have spoken God's word into my life and have encouraged me in the faith.

Also to my beloved wife Margaret, whose consistent love and faithfulness have enabled us together, to fulfill the calling on our lives. Also to our dear children, Susannah and Daniel, although now grown up and making their own way in life, came with us as small children, leaving friends and a place that they were familiar with to embark on this journey of faith with us to Anglesey.

Most of all I want to acknowledge the grace and mercy of God my Father that He has shown to me from my earliest days, to Jesus Christ, my Lord and Savior and to the Holy Spirit to whom belongs all credit and praise.

Chapter 1

WHAT IS CONFESSION?

When church people talk about confession, they often think of confessing sin. This is important, but it is not the only kind of confession that the Bible speaks of. The word *confess* actually means "to say the same as," so although it is important to agree with God about what sin is and how we have all fallen short of the standard that He has for us, we also need to see that, as born again believers in Jesus Christ, we now have a new identity. It is extremely important, therefore, that we renew our minds according to the new life that we have received from Christ. God's word is the truth, but unless we change our thinking in line with that truth, we will always be living far short of the victorious life that He has for us.

> And do not be conformed to this world,
> but be transformed by the renewing of
> your mind, that you may prove what is

that good and acceptable and perfect will of God. (Romans 12:2)

As a man thinks in his heart, so is he. (Proverbs 23:7)

In Hebrew, the word for meditation can also be translated as "mutter," which means speaking aloud. Confessing God's word, therefore, is also a way of meditating on it. The Bible says a lot about meditation and the rewards that come with it.

This Book of the Law shall not depart from your mouth, but you shall meditate in it day and night, that you may observe to do according to all that is written it. For then you will make your way prosperous, and then you will have good success.

Have I not commanded you? Be strong and of good courage; do not be afraid, nor be dismayed, for the LORD your God is with you wherever you go. (Joshua 1: 8-9)

When we declare God's word over our lives (and the lives of others), we are meditating on it and exercising our faith in what God has said and our thinking changes. In doing this, we are aligning our lives with His truth and our minds begin to be renewed.

We begin the Christian life by confessing the truth that Jesus is Lord of our lives. So we must continue by confession of the truth.

> As you therefore have received Christ Jesus as Lord, so walk in Him. (Colossians 2: 6)

> Let us hold fast the confession of our hope without wavering, for He who promised is faithful. (Hebrews 10: 23)

Chapter 2

THE POWER OF CONFESSION

Confessing God's word is a very effective way of releasing God's power in our lives and circumstances. It is also a wonderful way of bringing our tongue and our minds under the control of the Holy Spirit. The tongue is the most unruly member of our body; if we can control it, we are perfect!

> For we all stumble in many things. If anyone does not stumble in word, he is a perfect man, able also to bridle the whole body. (James 3: 2)

James says that our tongues can be compared to the rudder of a ship in that though it is small, yet it gives direction to the whole ship.

> Look also at ship: although they are so large and are driven by fierce winds, they

are turned by a very small rudder wherever
the pilot desires.

Even so, the tongue is a little member and
boasts great things. See how great a forest
a little fire kindles! (James 3: 4-5)

Death and life are in the power of the
tongue. (Proverbs 18: 21)

Many Christians see themselves as being unworthy and
failures. There could be many reasons for this, depending
on their past experiences. They feel failures because they
have failed in the past and in many cases continue to speak
very negatively about themselves. This leads to a cycle of
defeated living which is not the plan and purpose of God
for our lives. Although we may have failed in the past in
various areas of our lives, God does not see us as failures.
We need to see things more like He does. How can we
do that? We can do that by confessing and declaring His
truth daily to renew our minds. Our thoughts will then
agree with the word of God.

Then Jesus said to those Jews who believed
Him, "If you abide in My word, you are
My disciples indeed. And you shall know
the truth, and the truth will make you
free." (John 8: 31-32)

As we understand what God has done for us and embrace it, our conversation will change. As our speaking changes, so our behavior will change because our minds will gradually be renewed according to God's truth.

In order to proceed and understand more about the daily confession, we will need to ask God for revelation. This will enable us to know rather than just believe! A good prayer for this is based on the one that Paul prayed for the Ephesian church. I have personalized it so that you can make it your own prayer. It is also good to pray it for others. You can say it as follows:

> Father God, the Father of glory and of our Lord Jesus Christ, grant me the spirit of wisdom and revelation in the knowledge of Him. May the eyes of my understanding be opened so that I will know what is the hope of His calling, what are the riches of the glory of His inheritance in the saints and what is the exceeding greatness of His power for me who believes, according to the working of His mighty power, which He worked in Christ when He raised Him from the dead and seated Him at His right hand in the heavenly places, far above all principality and power and might and dominion and every name that is named, not only in this age but also in

the age to come. I ask this in the name of
Jesus. Amen

The reason it is important to pray that prayer, is
because it is not using the power of positive thinking but
it is about receiving and declaring God's truth. It is by
knowing the truth that we can walk in freedom and the
truth has to be received by revelation from the Holy Spirit.
We know something that the Holy Spirit has revealed
to us as distinct from believing only with our intellect.
Knowing also involves a willingness to act on what we
believe.

God's word contains His power, and this is apparent
right at the beginning of creation when God spoke things
into existence.

Then God said, "Let there be light" and there was
light. (Genesis 1: 3)

> Then God said, "Let there be lights in the
> firmament of the heavens to divide the day
> from the night; and let them be for signs
> and seasons, and for days and years; "and
> let them be for lights in the firmament of
> the heavens to give light on the earth" and
> it was so. (Genesis 1: 14-15)

Jesus also illustrated this when He spoke and people
were healed or raised from the dead.

Then they brought to him one who was deaf and had an impediment in his speech, and they begged Him to put His hand on him.

And He took him aside from the multitude, and put his fingers in his ears, and He spat and touched his tongue.

Then, looking up to heaven, He sighed, and said to him, 'Ephphatha', that is, "Be opened."

Immediately his ears were opened, and the impediment of his tongue was loosed, and he spoke plainly. (Mark 7: 32-35)

Then He came, and touched the open coffin, and those who carried him stood still. And He said, "Young man, I say to you, arise,"

So he who was dead sat up and began to speak. And he presented him to his mother. (Luke 7: 14-15)

Now when He had said these things, He cried with a loud voice, "Lazarus come forth!"

> And he who had died came out bound
> hand and foot with grave clothes, and
> his face was wrapped with a cloth. Jesus
> said to them, "Loose him and let him go."
> (John 11: 43-44)

The Bible is a record of what God has said. We need, however, for the Holy Spirit to give us revelation, to make what the Bible says real in our lives. As we have revelation and declare God's truth over our lives, the Holy Spirit is able to bring it into being.

> (as it is written, "I have made you a father
> of many nations") in the presence of
> Him whom he believed - God, who gives
> life to the dead and calls those things
> which do not exist as though they did.
> (Romans 4: 17)

When we declare God's word in faith, it has creative power because the power is in the word. I have been privileged to see many miracles by declaring God's word in various situations.

There was the time in Nepal when a paralyzed man was brought into the service. He was a young man in his twenties and was carried in on a stretcher. He was not able to lift himself up without any help. I had been preaching about the lame man who was healed when Peter and John were on their way to the temple in Jerusalem to pray. I told them that Jesus Christ is alive and He can do the same things that He did in the Bible. At the end of the service, we prayed a prayer of authority and commanded healing. Many sick and needy people were there, and I was not sure what had happened to the young man. We encouraged him to come back to the service the following day because I didn't think that anything had happened to him. As I questioned my own faith concerning this young man and his healing, the following morning the Lord spoke to me very clearly through a verse in Jeremiah:

"Behold, I am the LORD, the God of all flesh. Is there anything too hard for Me?" (Jeremiah 32: 27)

After this, I knew God had given me the faith to pull the man up from his stretcher. In the service the following morning, during the worship, we gently pulled the man up and he started to walk! I found out later that he had experienced some healing on the first day. But at that time, I had not seen such a big miracle, so my faith needed a boost from the Lord before I was confident to pull him up. After he was walking on his own, people started crying because it was just like Jesus was there and we learned afterwards that the man was a Hindu. He was born-again very soon after this and now many years later he is a pastor of a church! To God be the glory!

Chapter 3

MY CONFESSION

I have been using these daily confessions, which are given at the end of the following chapters, over many years. They have helped me to renew my mind and to see myself more as God sees me, so that I can see His power demonstrated through me. My prayer is that they will do the same for you!

Some explanation is given for each one and then in Appendix 2, they are listed in such a way, as to make it easy for you to incorporate them into your daily devotions. It is by making these confessions a daily habit that there will be great benefit. Your mind will be renewed in line with God's thinking! This is not intended to be an over simplified solution to all problems, but it is part of the armor that God has given us and little by little we are changed.

The daily confessions are all based on the covenant names of God. In the Bible a name is associated with character so these covenant names of God are a revelation of His character. It is only as we get to know God that we can truly believe and trust Him. It is hard to trust someone if we are not convinced that they love us and have our best interests at heart. That is why there is emphasis on the names and the character of God. The more we get to know Him, the more we will love and trust Him. Throughout Scripture when God had chosen His covenant people the Jews, He revealed Himself to them according to their needs at various times. We can see from this that human need can only be completely met by a revelation of God Himself.

God called Moses to deliver the Israelites from the slavery they were in to Pharaoh when in Egypt. While Moses was looking after the flock of sheep belonging to Jethro his father-in-law, he had an encounter with God. During this encounter, the Lord told him to go to Pharaoh and that he would empower him to bring deliverance to the Israelites, who had been crying out to God because of the oppression of slavery they were suffering. Moses then asked the Lord a very interesting question and he received an even more interesting answer!

> Then Moses said to God, "Indeed, when I come to the children of Israel and say to them, 'The God of your fathers has sent me to you,' and they say to me, 'What is His name?' what shall I say to them?"

> And God said to Moses, "I AM WHO I
> AM." And He said, "Thus you shall say to
> the children of Israel, 'I AM has sent me
> to you.'" (Exodus 3:13-14)

The name *I AM* is a translation of four Hebrew letters known by scholars as the sacred tetragrammaton or *YHWH* in Latin script. It is a name so sacred that orthodox Jews would not say it and so no one knows exactly how it should be pronounced. It is also very difficult to translate accurately into English but it has been suggested that it could be translated as "always". Orthodox Jews will sometimes simply refer to it as *The Name* or they will change it to Adonai, which can also be translated as Lord. Many Bible translators when translating the sacred tetragrammaton into English will use capitals for LORD, so as to distinguish it from when translating the Hebrew word Adonai. The name Jehovah is an anglicized derivation of the Hebrew name YHWH.

In the Bible, a name generally depicts the character of the person who is given the name. For example "Jacob", whose name means "supplanter" had his name changed to Israel, meaning "man of God", when he met with the Lord at Peniel. The name Gideon means "mighty warrior" which is exactly what he became. The name Jesus or Yeshua in Hebrew means Savior, which is what He is. These covenant names of God describe the character of God and through getting to know and understand more about God's character we can more easily exercise faith in Him.

> Now the LORD descended in the cloud
> and stood with him there, and proclaimed
> the name of the LORD. (Exodus 34:5)

This is the name (LORD or YHWH) that God revealed to the Jewish people with whom He has made covenants, and for this reason it is often referred to as God's covenant name. It is important for us to see that as believers in Christ we are also His covenant people. This new covenant was prophesied about by Jeremiah.

> But this is the new covenant that I will
> make with the house of Israel after those
> days, says the LORD; I will put my law in
> their minds, and write it on their hearts;
> and I will be their God, and they shall be
> My people. (Jeremiah 31: 33)

Paul describes God's people as being like an olive tree, with the Jews being natural branches and the Gentile believers in Jesus, being wild branches that have been grafted in.

> And if some of the branches were broken
> off, and you, being a wild olive tree, were
> grafted in among them, and with them

a partaker of the root and fatness of the
olive tree. (Romans 11:17)

Gentile believers in Jesus can therefore together with
Jewish believers in Christ (the Messiah), partake of the
blessing of the new covenant which was originally given
to Israel. When we share the communion together as
believers we affirm this new covenant.

For this is My blood of the new covenant,
which is shed for many for the remission
of sins. (Matthew 26: 28)

The blood of Jesus that was poured out for us was the
outpouring of His life which was totally pure, sinless and
holy. His blood was accepted by the Father in exchange
for the judgment on sin that we deserved, and it enables us
to share in the new covenant. It is important for us to see,
therefore, that the confessions of God's word that we make
come from the God with whom we are in covenant. This
means that we can totally rely on God's covenant promises.

The Hebrew word for covenant used in the Bible is
berit and it has a much stronger meaning than a contract.
It is better defined as a solemn binding agreement between
two parties which was generally sealed with the shedding
of blood. There are at least five covenants which God
instigated in Scripture and the one made with Moses at
Sinai was conditional upon the obedience of the Israelites

to all the laws which God gave to them through Moses. The new covenant, however, is different because what the children of Israel could not do in keeping the laws, Christ did and we receive the benefits by grace and faith because of Christ's obedience.

> For by grace you have been saved through faith and that not of yourselves it is the gift of God. (Ephesians 2:8)

The teaching of the New Testament is clear, that the new covenant, which is ours through Christ, renders the covenant that God made with Moses and the Israelites at Sinai, obsolete. If you belong to Christ then these declarations of truth are yours because of the covenant that God has made with us and which has been sealed with the blood of Jesus.

These daily confessions are based on the covenant names of God and each one of them depicts a different aspect of God's character which is revealed to God's people at the time of a particular need. The covenant names, of which there are eight listed, cover every aspect of human need! This is part of the whole salvation that is ours in Christ.

They are described in the order which they occur in the Bible, and are set in context so that we can rightly relate to them. Other Scriptures are included which compliment the truth revealed in God's covenant name.

The confessions which can be used daily are listed at the end of each chapter and they are also listed together in Appendix 2 for convenience of use.

Chapter 4

YHWH JIREH - I AM THE LORD YOUR PROVIDER

Now it came to pass after these things that God tested Abraham, and said to him, "Abraham!" and he said, "Here I am."

Then He said, "Take now your son, your only son Isaac, whom you love, and go to the land of Moriah, and offer him there as a burnt offering on one of the mountains which I shall tell you."

So Abraham rose early in the morning and saddled his donkey, and took two of his young men with him, and Isaac his son; and he split the wood for the burnt offering, and arose and went to the place of which God had told him.

Then on the third day Abraham lifted his eyes and saw the place afar off.

And Abraham said to his young men, "Stay here with the donkey; the lad and I will go yonder and worship, and we will come back to you.

So Abraham took the wood of the burnt offering and laid it on Isaac his son; and he took the fire in his hand, and a knife, and the two of them went together.

But Isaac spoke to Abraham his father and said, "My father!" And he said, "Here I am, my son." Then he said, "Look the fire and the wood, but where is the lamb for a burnt offering?"

And Abraham said, "My son, God will provide for Himself the lamb for a burnt offering." So the two of them went together.

Then they came to the place of which God had told him. And Abraham but an altar there and placed the wood in order; and he bound Isaac his son and laid him on the altar, upon the wood.

And Abraham stretched out his hand and took the knife to slay his son.

But the Angel of the LORD called to him from heaven and said, "Abraham! Abraham!" So he said, "Here I am."

And He said, "Do not lay your hand on the lad, or do anything to him; for now I know that you fear God, since you have not withheld your son, your only son from Me."

Then Abraham lifted his eyes and looked, and there behind him was a ram caught in the thicket by its horns. So Abraham went and took the ram and offered it up for a burnt offering instead of his son.

And Abraham called the name of the place, The LORD-Will-Provide, as it is said to this day, "In the Mount of the LORD it shall be provided." (Genesis 22: 1-14)

Can we imagine what Abraham was going through; because Isaac was the miracle child they had waited so long for? Abraham and Sarah were unable to have children but the Lord gave them a promise when He spoke to Abraham about Sarah!

"And I will bless her and also give you a son
by her; then I will bless her, and she shall
be a mother of nations; kings of peoples
shall be from her." (Genesis 17: 16)

"Is anything too hard for the LORD? At
the appointed time I will return to you,
according to the time of life, and Sarah
shall have a son." (Genesis 18: 14)

Naturally speaking it was impossible and Sarah had
given Abraham her maid Hagar to have a child with her,
but that was not the way God had planned. Abraham
was a hundred and Sarah ninety when Isaac was born. In
the Bible when a barren wife gave birth miraculously to a
child, it was always for a special purpose. Other examples
are Isaac and Rebekah who gave birth to Jacob and Esau,
Hannah who gave birth to Samuel and Zechariah and
Elizabeth in the New Testament who gave birth to John
the Baptist. All these women had been barren.

God is still doing miracles like this today! In Nepal
more than ten years ago, as I was praying before speaking
at a conference, I sensed that the Lord showed me that
there would be a married couple in the meeting who
wanted to have a baby but were not able to. I announced
this in the service and a young couple responded and we
discovered that they had been trying to have a baby for four
years. Also, they loved children and looked after orphan

children for their pastor. At the service we laid hands on the couple, broke the curse of barrenness and blessed them in the name of Jesus. A year later on another visit, the local pastor introduced us to the couple who now had a three month old baby boy! Isn't the Lord amazing!

The miracle child Isaac grew and most likely he was a teenager when God told Abraham to offer him as a burnt offering. By this time Abraham's faith had grown because, as the letter to the Hebrews in the New Testament explains he believed that even if Isaac was killed, God would raise him from the dead. This is based on the fact that he told his servants that <u>they</u> would return (including Isaac). This is a picture of God the Father giving his only Son, Jesus to be an offering for our sin and He was raised from the dead.

When we think of the Lord being our Provider, we often thing of material things that we need including money but the provision that God has made for us is complete and covers every area of human need. If we consider the entirety of human need with all of the suffering and deprivation, God has provided one solution. That solution is the sacrificial death of Jesus Christ on the cross and the whole gospel message is based on this one historical even which took place in Jerusalem.

The account of Abraham and Isaac is a picture of that solution in which God has made complete provision for every area of our lives. The fundamental need of mankind is reconciliation with God. It is because of man's rebellion against God which began with Adam and Eve. This reconciliation could only take place if the rebellion was dealt with. The prophet Isaiah described that event 700 years before it happened:

> But He was wounded for our transgressions,
>
> He was bruised for our iniquities;
>
> The chastisement for our peace was upon Him,
>
> And by His stripes we are healed.
>
> All we like sheep have gone astray;
>
> We have turned every one, to his own way;
>
> And the Lord has laid on Him the iniquity of us all. (Isaiah 53: 5-6)

Another word for iniquity is rebellion, and this is what we have all inherited from Adam, who chose to disobey the Lord. In essence he handed the authority that God had given to him, over to Satan, which is why he is described as the prince of this world. Jesus is described in the Bible as the last Adam and where the first Adam failed Jesus was victorious. When Adam was tempted by Satan he fell, but when Jesus was temped He overcame! Abraham offering up his beloved son Isaac is for us a picture of God the Father giving His only beloved Son as a sinless sacrifice for us.

> "For God so loved the world that He gave His only begotten Son, that whoever believes in Him should not perish but have everlasting life. (John 3: 16)

When Jesus was crucified He was being punished as if He was the worst of criminals in that day. He was subject to open ridicule, mockery and shame, hanging naked on that cross. That was the punishment required to deal with our rebellion. His sinless life and the shedding of His precious blood were accepted by the Father in exchange for our sin. In doing this provision has been made so that we could be reconciled with God the Father.

The basic need for every human on the earth is for a relationship with God as our Father, from whom we were alienated by Adam's sin. However, once we are reconciled to the Lord we become His children and we must renew our minds to the truth that we are no longer poor.

> For you know the grace of our Lord Jesus Christ, that though He was rich, yet for your sakes He became poor, that you through His poverty might become rich. (2 Corinthians 8:9)

Jesus Christ became poor on the cross, when He was

stripped of everything. He became poor so that we might become rich. Being rich has nothing to do with how much money you earn or how much you have in your bank account. Rather it depends on who your Father is! It is how you see yourself.

Many years ago I was with my good friend Trevor Newport in Nepal, and we were teaching at church leaders seminars. Trevor, at the beginning of his talk, asked the leaders how many of them were poor. They all put their hands up! He then went on to teach them for about forty five minutes what the Bible says about us. Afterwards, he asked them again how many were poor. There were none! So, in forty five minutes he had made them all rich! If we see ourselves as poor we will always be begging but if we renew our minds to who we are in Christ we become givers.

Having received Jesus as Lord of our lives we are now reconciled to God as our Father. He takes care of us because we belong to Him, having been purchased by the precious blood of Christ. As we renew our minds to the fact that God has provided for us, and in Christ all our needs are met, then faith rises in our hearts to face any situation. We can also help others to come to the same place of faith. This confession is based on the revelation of God's character that He is our Provider, and other verses of Scripture are included which state the same truth, but in a personalized way. This is our position in Christ and it does not depend on our circumstances but by declaring the truth of God's word our circumstances can change. As we realize how blessed we are it will be much easier to be obedient to the Lord with our giving.

The context of the well-known verse in Philippians which is part of the confession is that the church had been in partnership with Paul supporting his apostolic ministry. So it is important that these confessions are accompanied by an obedient life to the word of God. Even as Abraham was obedient to offer up his son as a sacrifice, so we must emulate that same kind of obedience. It is important to say the personalized confessions out loud then you will hear them as well as speak them. They are based on Philippians 4: 19, Ephesians 1: 3 and Proverbs 10: 22

> YHWH Jireh – I Am the LORD Your Provider
>
> The Lord is My Provider
>
> And my God shall supply all my need according to His riches in glory by Christ Jesus.
>
> I am blessed with every spiritual blessing in heavenly places in Christ.
>
> The blessing of the Lord makes me rich and He adds no sorrow with it.

I declare today that I am blessed spiritually, intellectually, emotionally, physically, my family is blessed, my work is blessed, my ministry is blessed and my finances are

Chapter 5

YHWH ROPHE - I AM THE LORD WHO HEALS YOU

So Moses brought Israel from the Red Sea; then they went out into the wilderness of Shur. And they went three days in the wilderness and found no water.

Now when they came to Marah, they could not drink the waters of Marah, for they were bitter. Therefore the name of it as called Marah.

And the people complained against Moses, saying, "What shall we drink?" So he cried out to the LORD and the LORD showed him a tree. When he cast it into the waters, the waters were made sweet.

There He made a statute and an ordinance for them, and there He tested them,

and said, "If you diligently heed the voice of the LORD your God and do what is right in His sight, give ear to His commandments and keep all His statutes, I will put none of the diseases on you which I have brought on the Egyptians. For I am the LORD who heals you." (Exodus 15: 22-26)

Immediately before this in the text, the Israelites were singing victory songs! They had seen the Lord deliver them from the Egyptians with so many miraculous signs but now they are being tested and after three days of journeying in the wilderness they cannot find any water! When they did find some they were not able to drink it because it was bitter (possibly some would have been made sick attempting to drink it). Water is essential for life and the situation must have looked very bleak. The miracles which had occurred just days earlier must have seemed to be in the distant past.

It is remarkable how we can slip, from a great victory to defeat in a very short space of time. Peter had this experience, one moment he had received the revelation that Jesus is the Messiah, the Son of the living God but the next Jesus had to rebuke him because he hadn't understood that Jesus had to go to the cross.

Sadly, this happened with the Israelites, a mountain top experience with God to a valley of temptation in a very short space of time. They were being tested and the Lord clearly wanted them to trust Him in the situation. As is often said, a test is an opportunity for a testimony, if we will maintain a good attitude. We all have such opportunities, but the key is to stay in faith and we can do this by keeping in mind His promises. Complaining is regarded very seriously in Scripture by the Lord, because it reveals a heart of unbelief. It is this unbelief and disobedience that kept this generation of Israelites from entering the Promised Land. It is similar with us, unbelief and disobedience will keep us from experiencing God's best for our lives. Regularly feeding and meditating on God's word will help us not to regress into unbelief.

The Lord gave me revelation from the Scriptures about healing many years ago and if I was attacked by sickness in my body I would rebuke it and confess healing scriptures over my life. There was a good measure of success but one day I was hit with a really bad dose of the flu and just could not shake it off. Reluctantly I gave in and went to bed. I asked the Lord why my prayers were not working, and He reminded me very quickly that some time before I had promised the Lord that I would take a day off work to spend time with Him in prayer, but had not done so. As soon as I confessed my disobedience and resolved to put it right I felt an immediate improvement in my physical condition. My disobedience had made an entrance for sickness.

The Lord was very kind to the Israelites and as they complained, Moses cried out to the Lord. In response, the Lord showed him a tree which he was to cast into the waters. The bitter waters then became potable and the thirsty Israelites could drink. This is a picture for us of the cross of Christ, as that is what the tree represents.

> Christ has redeemed us from the curse of
> the law, having become a curse for us (for it
> is written, "Cursed is everyone who hangs
> on a tree"), (Galatians 3: 13)

The cross of Christ is God's remedy for every need there is in this sin sick world. By one event in history, God demonstrated His love for suffering humanity and provided a solution. Every human being has inherited alienation from God due to Adam and Eve's disobedience. Sickness and disease are a consequence of this alienation. The cross, however is the remedy and Isaiah prophesied about it seven hundred years before the event,

> Surely He has borne our griefs
> And carried our sorrows;
> Yet we esteemed Him stricken,
> Smitten by God, and afflicted.

> But He was wounded for our transgressions,
> He was bruised for our iniquities;
> The chastisement for our peace was upon Him,
> And by His stripes we are healed.
> All we like sheep have gone astray;
> We have turned everyone to his own way;
> And the Lord has laid on Him the iniquity
> of us all. (Isaiah 53: 4-6)

When Jesus was healing the sick and casting out demons the gospel writer Mathew states:

> that it might be fulfilled which was spoken
> by Isaiah the prophet, saying;

> "He Himself took our infirmities and bore
> our sicknesses." (Matthew 8: 17)

There is therefore no doubt that Isaiah 53 refers to physical healing, in fact the Hebrew word translated "griefs" is the word used for sickness even today in modern Hebrew and the Hebrew word translated "sorrows" can also be translated as pain. The cross of Jesus is the answer for all of our needs including the physical and emotional. We can suffer from sorrow due to bereavement, broken relationships or from disappointments due to our own actions or the actions of others. We are not suggesting that with bereavement, for example, there is not a natural process of grieving to go through because the Scripture does acknowledges this in many places. However grief, (whatever the cause) should not take such root, that it becomes a destructive force in our loves. There is healing for the broken hearted!

> "The Spirit of the LORD is upon Me,
> Because He has anointed Me
> To preach the gospel to the poor;
> He has sent Me to heal the broken hearted,
> To proclaim liberty to the captives
> And recovery of sight to the blind,
> To set at liberty those who are oppressed;
> To proclaim the acceptable year of the
> LORD." (Luke 4:18-19)

We do not have all the answers regarding healing and we should certainly never criticize people who are sick, but rather pray for them. Although there can be many reasons why people are sick, there are however certain principles in Scripture which are necessary for us to understand, if we are to see healings take place on a regular basis. The first is that it is in the character of God to heal, which means that He wants to heal sick people. It is hard for someone to receive healing from the Lord, if they are not sure that he wants them well. The Bible gives us the revelation of God's will. His promises to Israel, to the church and the ministry of Jesus make it abundantly clear that it is God's will to heal.

There are clearly many ways that we can receive healing and there are also many causes for sickness. Our lifestyle is important, what we eat and drink and how we look after our bodies. Learning to live in the peace of God is important, as stress can cause so many physical problems. It is not within the scope of this book to go into too much detail because there are many good books written on the subject of healing. Confessing the truth of God's word concerning healing, however, certainly helps to keep us in health. It is better to stay healthy than to keep getting sick and being healed. God's word is like a medicine which needs to be taken on a regular basis.

> My son, give attention to my words;
> incline your ear to my sayings.
> Do not let them depart from your eyes;
> Keep them in the midst of your heart;
> For they are life to those who find them,
> And health to all their flesh. (Proverbs 4: 20-22)

There can be no question here that these verses speak about healing in our bodies because a specific reference is made to health to the flesh. Also there is a clear link between meditating on God's word and healing. Confessing healing Scriptures is a great way to meditate on God's word because the word is spoken but it is also heard and so imparts faith.

Healing can also be a sign to unbelievers when preaching the gospel. In our ministry in Asia and Africa particularly, we have seen thousands come to Christ in situations where they have also seen the Lord heal.

> And they went out and preached everywhere, the Lord working with them and confirming the word through the accompanying signs. Amen. (Mark 16: 20)

I heard about a church recently that had healing groups to minister to sick people. They had been trained not to pray conventionally over the people but simply to declare the truths of God's word over them and they saw amazing results. Before they would minister to others, they met together and declared the same Scriptures over their own lives. The pastor reported how it was very rare for anyone in the church to get sick during that period!

As has been mentioned there are many ways for people to receive healing, but renewing our minds and filling our hearts with God's word helps us to stay healthy, and to walk closer to Him.

The gifts of the Holy Spirit are another means whereby people can receive healing.

One time in our church, we had advertised healing meetings, and at one of these I announced that I believed that the Lord had shown me that there was someone there who had severe pain in their back. A young lady responded and as we laid hands on her she said with a glowing face, "I think that I am growing!" We discovered later, that when she was fourteen she had a horse riding accident, and damaged her shoulder. In fact, it had not healed properly and the upshot was that she, in trying to walk uprightly had put a lot a pressure on her back which was the cause of the pain. The Lord, knowing this dealt with the cause of the problem, and not just the symptom. However, even though the problem was revealed through a word of knowledge we still confessed God's word over the lady when we laid hands on her.

When people receive healing in such a way, it is still important that they learn to confess God's word over their own lives so that they can stay healed. The confessions of God's word have been personalized are as follows. They are based on Isaiah 53: 5, Psalm 107: 20 and Psalm 103: 2 – 3 and are to be spoken with faith and confidence.

> YHWH Rophe - I Am the LORD Your Healer
>
> The Lord is my healer.
>
> The chastisement for our peace was upon Him and by His stripes we are healed.

The chastisement for my peace was upon Him and by His stripes I am healed.

By his stripes I was healed.

Since by His stripes I was healed then by His stripes I am healed.

Since by His stripes I am healed then I am healed!

He sent forth His word and He healed them.

He sent forth His word and He healed me.

Since He sent forth His word and healed me then I am healed!

Bless the Lord O my soul and all that is within me bless His holy name.

He has forgiven all your sins and He has healed all your diseases.

He has forgiven all my sins and He has healed all my diseases.

Since He has healed all my diseases then I am healed!

Chapter 6

YHWH NISSI - I AM THE LORD YOUR BANNER

Now Amalek came and fought with Israel in Rephidim.

> And Moses said to Joshua, "Choose us
> some men and go out, fight with Amalek.
> Tomorrow I will stand on the top of the
> hill with the rod of God in my hand."

> So Joshua did as Moses said to him, and
> fought with Amalek. And Moses, Aaron
> and Hur went up to the top of the hill.

> And so it was, when Moses held up his
> hand, that Israel prevailed; and when he
> let down his hand, Amalek prevailed.

But Moses' hands became heavy; so they took a stone and put it under him, and he sat on it. And Aaron and Hur supported his hands, one on one side, and the other on the other side, and his hands were steady until the going down of the sun.

So Joshua defeated Amalek and his people with the edge of the sword.

Then the people said to Moses, "Write this for a memorial in the book and recount it in the hearing of Joshua, that I will utterly blot out the remembrance of Amalek under heaven."

And Moses built an altar and called its name, The-LORD-is-My-Banner, (Exodus 17: 8-15)

Amalek was a grandson of Esau, and so the Amalekites were his descendants after him. Esau had taken wives from the daughters of Canaan, causing distress to his parents Isaac and Rebekah. This meant that his family would be no different to the other descendants of Canaan, who worshipped false gods and not the God of Israel. Now, the Amalekites are making an unprovoked attack against

Israel on their journey through the wilderness, which was abhorrent to God and the Israelites.

Moses instructs Joshua, his younger assistant, to select some fighting men to go out and confront the Amalekite enemy. Moses goes to the top of the hill, where he will be able to look down and see the progress of the battle with the rod of God in his hand. This tells us that Moses wasn't relying on the strength of his fighting men, but on the Lord, because this rod of God was the same rod that the Lord had given him to defeat Pharoah with. This rod represented the authority that God had given him and with it he parted the Red Sea for the Israelites to cross over on dry land. In Christ we have authority over our enemies!

Then He called His twelve disciples together and gave them power and authority over all demons, and to cure diseases. (Luke 9: 1)

> Which he worked in Christ when He raised Him from the dead and seated Him at His right hand in the heavenly places,
>
> far above all principality and power and might and dominion, and every name that is named, not only in this age but also in that which is to come.

And He put all things under His feet, and gave Him to be head over all things to the church,

which is His body, the fullness of Him who fills all in all. (Ephesians 1: 20-23)

But God, who is rich in mercy, because of His great love with which He loved us,

even when we were dead in trespasses, made us alive together with Christ (by grace you have been saved),

and raised us up together, and made us sit together in the heavenly places in Christ Jesus. (Ephesians 2: 4-6)

When we confess the truth of God's word, we do so with the authority that has been given to us in Christ. We declare the Scriptures with confidence, knowing that we are backed up by God Himself. When a policemen stands at a traffic junction and raises his hand, the traffic stops because they recognize the authority that he is acting under. In himself he has no power to stop all the vehicles that are in front of him, but the uniform and the badge is like the rod that Moses had.

There have been times in Nepal when we have been ministering to people and then we suddenly realize that demons are manifesting! The interesting thing is that even though the person we are ministering to does not understand English, when we issue a command with authority to the demon, then it goes. The demons recognize authority, so it is important that we have an understanding of God's word and the confidence to declare it.

Another lesson from the story is that there is a team effort. Aaron and Hur supported Moses, and when we have spiritual battles, it is always good to know that we have friends who can stand with us and know how to exercise authority with us. The Christian life was never meant to be a solitary one, because we are part of the body of Christ and so we need each other. This particularly applies to those in the front lines of the battle which is why we are told to pray especially for all those who are in positions of leadership.

We are told that Joshua defeated Amalek with the edge of the sword. God's word is likened to a sword as it is called the sword of the Spirit.

> And take the helmet of salvation, and the
> sword of the Spirit which is the word of
> God. (Ephesians 6: 17)

Jesus showed us how to overcome the enemy when we are attacked. In the wilderness when He was tempted by Satan, every time He overcame by declaring Scripture. In other words, He used the sword of the Spirit.

Another way to overcome the enemy is with praise and worship. This is often illustrated in Scripture, for example when Jehoshaphat, King of Judah was faced with a great multitude coming to attack, he sent out the singers to praise and worship the Lord ahead of the army, who didn't even need to fight because the Lord fought for them and defeated the enemy! There is power in praise!

> Now when they began to sing and to praise, the Lord set ambushes against the people of Ammon, Moab and Mount Seir, who had come up against Judah; and they were defeated. (2 Chronicles 20: 22)

Praise and worship is a way of using the sword of the Spirit in song and it is very powerful. As the word of God is declared, the Lord manifests His presence.

> But you are holy,
>
> Enthroned in the praises of Israel. (Psalm 22:3)

One time on a mission trip in Nepal we were very privileged to meet a pastor who had been among the first group of Nepalese to receive Christ in the 1960's. He had a small group of new believers who would meet secretly in his home because there was a lot of persecution against Christians. He wanted to reach his village with the gospel so he decided to organize a meal and invited the whole village to attend. The plan was that they would enjoy the meal then he would share the gospel with them. They came and in the middle of the proceedings some drunken soldiers arrived and threatened to kill them. The pastor remembered what he had read about Jehoshaphat and asked his small group of believers to sing some praise songs. They did and the soldiers started arguing among themselves and gradually drifted away! There is power in praise!

> Let the high praises of God be in their mouth,
>
> And a two-edged sword in their hands, (Psalm 149: 6)

It is a characteristic of Hebrew writing to make a point and then to repeat the same point but using different words. It is particularly noticeable in Psalm 149.

> Let Israel rejoice in their Maker;
>
> Let the children of Zion be joyful in their King. (Psalm 149: 2)

Israel rejoicing in their Maker is one and the same as the children of Zion being joyful in their King! We can see therefore, that when the high praises of God are in their mouths, it is the same as the two-edged sword in their hands. It has the same effect, which is to bring victory to the people of God.

In the letters to the seven churches in the book of Revelation there are rewards only for those who overcome.

To him who overcomes I will give to eat from the tree of life, which is in the midst of the paradise of God. (Revelation 2: 7)

He who overcomes shall not be hurt by the second death. (Revelation 2: 11)

To him who overcomes I will give some of the hidden manna to eat. And I will give him a white stone, and on the stone a new name written which no one knows except him who receives it. (Revelation 2: 17)

And he who overcomes, and keeps My works until the end, to him I will give power over the nations- (Revelation 2:26)

He who overcomes shall be clothed in white garments, and I will not blot his name from the Book of Life; but I will confess his name before My Father and before His angels. (Revelation 3: 5)

> He who overcomes, I will make him a pillar in the temple of My God- (Revelation 3:12)

> To him who overcomes I will grant to sit with Me on My throne, as I also overcame and sat down with My Father on His throne. (Revelation 3: 21)

We are called to overcome, but the good news is that Christ has done this for us and He calls us to share His victory. For this to be real in our lives we must renew our minds by having God's word living in our hearts.

> I have written to you, young men,

> Because you are strong, and the word of God abides in you,

> And you have overcome the wicked one. (1 John 1:4)

The confessions provided below if used regularly will help you to have God's word abiding in you. They are based on 1 Chronicles 18: 13, 1 Corinthians 15: 57 and Romans 8: 37 and they have been personalized.

> YHWH Nissi - I Am the LORD Your Banner

The Lord is my banner, the One who gives me victory.

I have total victory in Christ.

The Lord gives me victory everywhere I go.

I am more than a conqueror through Christ who strengthens me.

Chapter 7

YHWH SHALOM - I AM
THE LORD YOUR PEACE

So Gideon built an altar there to the
LORD, and called it The LORD is Peace.
(Judges 6: 24)

Gideon was an Israelite from the tribe of Manasseh, and
at this time Israel was being oppressed by the Midianites.
Their produce was being destroyed and so Israel was
impoverished, as well as being defeated in battle. The
Israelites had resorted to hiding in dens and caves in the
mountains. This was a very low season in Israel's history
and the prospects looked extremely bleak. They did the
right thing, however, when they turned to the only One
who could help!

> So Israel was greatly impoverished because
> of the Midianites, and the children of
> Israel cried out to the LORD. (Judges 6:6)

How sad that things have to go seriously wrong sometimes before we obey the Lord. If we turned to Him and obeyed Him earlier then maybe we could avoid some of the difficulties that come our way! There will, however, always be trouble in this life and being a Christian certainly does not exempt us from it. The Bible is clear that those who are intent on being true disciples of Jesus will have opposition but there are also times when the trouble is because of our own actions.

The Lord responded to Israel's cry for help by sending a prophet to speak to them. He reminds them about the miracles that He did for them in delivering them from slavery to the Egyptians and then tells them that they have not been obedient. Very often it's only when we hear a preacher that we realize that we have drifted away from God's plan for our lives and need to turn back. To see situations turn around we need faith and that comes as we hear God's word.

> How then shall they call on Him in whom
> they have not believed? And how shall
> they believe in Him of whom they have not
> heard? And how shall they hear without a
> preacher? (Romans 10: 14)

So then faith comes by hearing and hearing
by the word of God.(Romans 10: 17)

The next stage of God's deliverance plan in bringing
about the answer to the Israelites prayers occurs when
Lord appears to Gideon. At the time Gideon was
threshing wheat in a winepress. This is not the usual place
for threshing wheat but Gideon is hiding because of the
Midianite raiders. Along with other Israelites, Gideon was
discouraged and could see no way out of the situation. The
Lord appears to him and calls him, "a mighty warrior."

And the Angel of the LORD appeared to
him, and said to him, "The LORD is with
you, you mighty man of valor!" (Judges
6: 12)

This is very significant, because the words that
Gideon heard from the Lord were totally contrary to the
circumstances and to everything that he felt about himself
and the Israelites. He must have felt anything but a mighty
warrior! However this is characteristic of the Lord, who
speaks and things come into existence.

(as it is written, "I have made you a father
of many nations") in the presence of Him
whom he believed - God, who gives life
to the dead and calls those things which

do not exist as though they did. (Romans
4: 17)

The Lord did the same with Abraham when he and
his wife were unable to have children; He changes his
name from Abram to Abraham which means the father
of many nations! The Lord delights in allowing us to be
in situations where we have to trust Him to do miracles,
and then He gets the glory! When we say "I'm not....." He
says, "I Am....." Paul understood this and explained it to
the church in Corinth:

> Therefore I take pleasure in infirmities,
> in reproaches, in needs, in persecutions,
> in distresses, for Christ's sake. For when I
> am weak, then I am strong. (2 Corinthians
> 12: 10)

Gideon starts to discuss his dilemma with the Lord
and speaks very negatively about his situation. The Lord
completely ignores his negativity and continues to speak
faith to him and tells him that he is going to save Israel!
The Lord doesn't respond to our unbelief but to our faith.

> Gideon said to Him, "O my Lord, if the
> Lord is with us, why then has all this
> happened to us? And where are all His
> miracles which our fathers told us about
> saying, 'Did not the Lord bring us up from

Egypt?' But now the Lord has forsaken
us and delivered us into the hands of the
Midianites."

Then the Lord turned to him and said, "Go
in this might of yours and you shall save
Israel from the hand of the Midianites.
Have I not sent you?" (Judges 6: 13-14)

The Lord is very gracious, because as Gideon explained
how weak he and his tribe were, the Lord reassures him
that He is going with him, and that he will defeat the
Midianites. Each time Gideon brings up an objection, the
Lord speaks faith to him and assures him that He is going
to be involved. There are so many similarities with Moses,
who felt the same inadequacy.

Before the Lord can send him, however, he needs to
change him further. First he is speaking faith to him and
next he lets Gideon see His miracle power first hand.
Gideon brought an offering of a young goat to the Lord
and according to the instructions of the Lord, laid the goat
on a rock. The Lord then cause fire to come out of the rock
and consume the meat. This experience changed Gideon
as he now saw for himself the power of God.

Then the Angel of the Lord put out the
end of the staff that was in His hand, and
touched the meat and the unleavened

bread; and fire rose out of the rock and consumed the meat and the unleavened bread. And the Angel of the Lord departed out of his sight.

Now Gideon perceived that He was the Angel of the Lord. So Gideon said, "Alas, O Lord God! For I have seen the Angel of the Lord face to face."

Then the Lord said to him, "Peace be with you, do not fear, you shall not die."

So Gideon built an altar there to the Lord and called it The- LORD- Is- Peace. (Judges 6: 21-24)

An encounter with the Lord changes everything! This was my experience growing up in a gospel preaching church, my knowledge of God was head knowledge and when I arrived at university I met up with Christians who knew the Lord in a way which I didn't. I remember going to church one Sunday morning in Manchester where I was studying, with two fellow students. A man in the church, who had spoken to us previously, came up to us and said that God had shown him that he should pray for us every day. That statement had an amazing impact on me, because I hadn't realized that such a relationship with the Lord was available, where He actually showed people things and spoke to them.

In the church there were also people who prophesied and some of these prophecies seemed to be aimed directly at me! All this showed me that God knew about me and had a purpose for my life. It was during this time that I dedicated my life to Him and had an encounter with God that changed me forever.

One day I was reading a book about the Holy Spirit and I came across a verse from the book of Psalms:

> I am the Lord your God,
>
> Who brought you out of the land of Egypt;
>
> Open your mouth wide, and I will fill it.
> (Psalm 81: 10)

When I read this verse, I had a distinct sense that I should open my mouth and speak. Then out of my mouth flowed this language that I had never learned. I had been prayed for previously to receive the baptism in the Holy Spirit but this was now a few weeks later. At the same time I felt that my bedroom, where I was sitting, was filled with God's love and that I was being filled with God's love. I remember having a sense of such peace and security and thinking that even if there was an earthquake and the house fell down, it didn't matter because the Lord was with me!

From that time on, whenever I read the Bible it was just like God as speaking directly to me. The Lord was so real and He gave me a confidence that I didn't have before. I knew I was forgiven and loved by the Lord. That experience enabled me to believe with my heart rather than just my head.

This is the kind of faith that the Bible speaks of and enables people to do great exploits for God. Gideon was such a man, but before the Lord could use him, He had to bring him to a place of faith. Once Gideon knew the Lord personally, he saw himself in a different light and his conversation changed. No more was he so negative but he had confidence to believe that things were going to change. He too had an experience of the Holy Spirit.

> But the Spirit of the Lord came upon Gideon, then he blew the trumpet, and the Abiezrites gathered behind him. (Judges 6: 34)

People will follow someone who has confidence, and can inspire others with faith and hope. It is important to continue in faith and not to slip back into negativity. This is why regularly feeding on and meditating on God's word is so important.

This confession is based on Philippians 4: 6 – 7 and is personalized. It should be remembered that to refuse to worry is a decision that we must make and it takes no longer or anymore energy to sit and worry than it does to speak God's word over our lives! As you say it give any cares and burdens to the Lord and by faith receive His peace. You can say it several times so that the truth is established in your heart.

> YHWH Shalom - I Am the LORD Your Peace
>
> The Lord is my peace.
>
> I will in nothing be anxious, but I will in everything by prayer with supplication and thanksgiving let my requests be made known unto God and the peace of God which surpasses all understanding will guard my heart and mind through Christ Jesus.

Chapter 8

YHWH MAKADESH - I AM THE LORD WHO SANCTIFIES YOU

And you shall keep My statutes, and perform them: I am the LORD who sanctifies you. (Leviticus 20: 8)

Moreover I also gave them My Sabbaths, to be a sign between them and Me, that they might know that I am the LORD who sanctifies them. (Ezekiel 20: 12)

Ezekiel was from the priestly tribe of Levi; he was also a descendant of Zadok the priest and was born in 622 BC, at another very low point in Israel's history. About a hundred years before Ezekiel, the ten tribes of Israel had been carried off to Assyria and the prophets Amos and Hosea had been warning them for a long time about their disobedience, but they had ignored such warnings. When

Ezekiel was aged twenty five, he was deported to Babylon along with Daniel and other promising young men from the Jewish society.

When Ezekiel was thirty, he should have started his priesthood, but without a temple and far from Jerusalem, he couldn't ever be a priest in Babylon. However, it was at this time that he was called by God to be a prophet. He was mainly concerned with the two tribes Judah and Benjamin. Although they had observed what happened to the remaining tribes of Israel in the north, Judah also ignored the prophets that God sent to them.

There had been some high points in Judah's history, for example under kings such as Jehoshaphat and Josiah who brought about reforms but most of the kings were bad. Their behavior became more and more godless, so prophets such as Isaiah and Micah warned of judgment to come. Jeremiah came later and his warnings also were rejected.

The kings of Israel became puppet kings to the stronger nations of Egypt in the south and Babylon in the northeast. The last puppet king of Judah was Zedekiah, and for a time he was allowed to rule in Jerusalem. When Jerusalem was invaded, he was taken as a prisoner by the army of the Babylonian King Nebuchadnezzar. The Babylonian soldiers killed Zedekiah's sons in front of him and then blinded him! This was the backdrop to which Ezekiel was called to preach in Babylon! It was also at this time that the Jews learned to speak Aramaic which was the language of the Babylonians.

Like Moses and others before him, Ezekiel had some amazing encounters with God. His calling was not an easy one! However, like the apostles Paul and John, because he experienced God in such a powerful way and saw into Heaven, he was sustained through all the trials that he endured. Ezekiel was called to a people that the Lord described as impudent, stubborn and rebellious! What a calling! He was warned not to become like them neither should he be afraid of them.

The name Ezekiel means "God strengthens" and he certainly needed God's strength in order to fulfill his ministry. For the first three years of Ezekiel's ministry in Babylon he prophesied that Jerusalem would be completely destroyed. At this time, although Jerusalem was under Babylon's control it hadn't yet been destroyed.

His prophecy came to pass in 587 BC and it also at the same time his wife died. Ezekiel's life, as well as his words was a prophetic sign for the people to see how God was feeling about the consequences of their actions. As Ezekiel had lost the wife that he loved, so the Lord had lost connection with the city and the people that He loved. The Lord instructed Ezekiel to communicate in this visual way on many occasions. The first time, he was to take a clay tablet with the city of Jerusalem portrayed on it under siege and with battering rams against it on every side.

Ezekiel was called to warn God's people of the

consequences of their sin and that of their fathers. The sins of Judah had persisted for a long time, and some of the worst, and perhaps the most offensive to God was the idolatry that had gone on in the temple. The temple was built in King Solomon's reign and was for the worship of the one true and living God, the God of Israel. It was a place where the glory of God appeared but now that glory had departed and it was important that God's people understood why.

They had been worshipping the goddess Asherah in the temple! Women were also sitting at the north gate of the temple worshipping the goddess Tamuz! In vision Ezekiel also about twenty five men at the door of the temple, between the porch and the altar facing the east and worshipping the sun! Ezekiel makes it clear that the prophets, priests and the kings were largely responsible for the state of Jerusalem.

Idolatry was not their only sin; there was also much immorality, exploitation of the vulnerable, such as widows and orphans as well as murders. The Ten Commandments had been broken, without any sign of repentance and now they were reaping the consequences. Ezekiel was a man who had to live in a very close relationship with the Lord, because his message was not a popular one that everybody wanted to hear. It was through his relationship with the Lord that he as sustained and this is a great example for us.

If we will stay in close fellowship with the Lord then, whatever trials or persecutions befall us, the Lord is able to bring us through. When I met with God in a very powerful as a university student, the Lord became so real to me. To be able to hear God's voice and know that God was speaking to me on different occasions has sustained me through the tests and trials of life.

Ezekiel's message was certainly not all gloom and doom. He truly revealed God's character and heart by demonstrating that, because of His great love, He would restore His people. There are glimpses of this in the earlier chapters but most of the restoration prophecies are recorded in the latter part of the book. Jeremiah also had prophesied the restoration of the Jews to the land:

> For thus says the Lord. After seventy years are completed at Babylon, I will visit you and perform My good word toward you, and cause you to return to this place.
>
> For I know the thoughts that I think toward you, says the Lord, thoughts of peace and not of evil, to give you a future and a hope.
>
> Then you will call upon Me and go and pray to Me, and I will listen to you. (Jeremiah 29: 10-12)

These prophets revealed the heart of God which was to bring healing and restoration. This is illustrated in the gospel message that God is holy, and sin cannot just be overlooked but because of His great love, Jesus Christ came and endured rejection, pain, hostility, mockery and all the sufferings of crucifixion for us.

> "For God so loved the world that He gave His only begotten Son, that whoever believes in Him should not perish but have everlasting life.
>
> For God did not send His Son into the world to condemn the world, but that the world through Him might be saved.
>
> He who believes in Him is not condemned; but he who does not believe is condemned already, because he has not believed in the name of the only begotten Son of God. (John 3: 16-18)
>
> The Lord is not slack concerning His promise, as some count slackness, but is longsuffering toward us, not willing that any should perish but that all should come to repentance.(2 Peter 3:9)

This is God's heart which is revealed through the prophets like Ezekiel and in the New Testament.

In the early years of Ezekiel's ministry in Babylon,

when he was required to make known to the people of Judah the abominations of their fathers, even here there is a hint of hope.

> "Moreover I also gave them My Sabbaths, to be a sign between them and Me, that they might know that I am the LORD who sanctifies them. (Ezekiel 20: 12)

The Lord was reminding Ezekiel of the time much earlier when Moses was giving the Law to the Israelites in Sinai.

> Then the Lord spoke to Moses, saying,

> "Speak also to the children of Israel, saying: 'Surely My Sabbaths you shall keep, for it is a sign between Me and you throughout your generations, that you may know that I am the LORD who sanctifies you. (Exodus 31: 12-13)

One of the distinguishing marks of the Jewish people down through the centuries has been Sabbath keeping and this has been a sign that they belong to the Lord. The word "sanctify" is a word which is not used much outside of church circles but it simply means "to be set apart". God had set apart Israel for Himself and had instructed them to keep His Sabbaths as a sign that they belonged to Him.

The word 'saint' is related to the word "sanctify", in that a "saint" is someone who has been set apart by the Lord.

When Paul writes to the church in Corinth he addresses them as saints, meaning that they were a people who once were worshipping other gods or no god, but now they have given their lives to Christ and so are set apart for Him. The Corinthian church did not, in many cases, act like saints but nevertheless it was their calling.

It is the same with us, and it was the same with Gideon, God calls us what He plans for us to become. Of course, it may take time, but He empowers us and does not leave us to change in our own strength. In Exodus and Leviticus sanctification is linked with the keeping of the Sabbath and the writer to the Hebrews explains more about what this means to believers in Christ.

> For He has spoken in a certain place of the seventh day in this way: "And God rested on the seventh day from all His works." (Hebrews 4: 4)

> There remains therefore a rest for the people of God.

> For he who has entered His rest has himself also ceased from his own works as God did from His. (Hebrews 4: 9-10)

There is a place of rest with God, in this life. It is a

place where we are fully trusting Him and not trying in our own strength to work for Him. We have our part to play but that is to cooperate with Him and to obey Him. There are times when the Holy Spirit searches our hearts and reveals that our motives are selfish or our reactions to people or circumstances are not right and it is at such times that we come to the cross and experience cleansing again. There is the truth then, that we are being sanctified as well as having been sanctified. We are set apart for the Lord but He is gradually changing us as we walk with Him.

> Search me, O God and know my heart;
>
> Try me and know my anxieties;
>
> And see if there be any wicked way in me,
>
> And lead me in the way everlasting. (Psalm 139: 23-24)
>
> But if we walk in the light as He is in the light, we have fellowship with one another and the blood of Jesus Christ His Son cleanses us from all sin. (1 John 1: 7)

We begin by trusting Him for forgiveness and His acceptance not putting any reliance on our own good works. We must then continue to trust Him for holiness and sanctification by allowing Christ to have His way in our lives. We repent when we are wrong and learn to live in His grace and mercy.

> "Come unto Me, all you who labor and are heavy laden, and I will give you rest.
>
> "Take my yoke upon you and learn from Me, for I am gentle and lowly in heart, and you will find rest for your souls.
>
> "For My yoke is easy and My burden is light." (Matthew 11: 28-29)

Jesus was speaking of the rest of faith that comes from trusting Him and walking in relationship with Him, as opposed to trying to keep hundreds of laws by our own efforts.

The confession related to this revelation of God's character is personalized and affirms these truths. They should be said slowly and thoughtfully. They are based on 1 Thessalonians 5: 23, Philippians 1: 21 and Galatians 2: 20

> YHWH Makedesh - I Am the LORD who Sanctifies You
>
> The Lord is my sanctifier

And now the God of peace will sanctify me completely, my whole, spirit, soul and body.

For me to live is Christ.

Christ lives in me.

Father God, today I receive from You all that I need to live for You. Forgiveness and cleansing by the blood of Jesus and a fresh infilling of the Holy Spirit to captivate my heart. Let Your refining fire go through my heart, burn out anything that is not pleasing to You, set my heart ablaze with love and passion for You. I offer to You my spirit, soul and body to be set apart for You. For Your glory.

Chapter 9

YHWH ROHI - I AM THE LORD YOUR SHEPHERD

The Lord is my shepherd;
I shall not want.
He makes me to lie down in green pastures;
He leads me beside the still waters.
He restores my soul;
He leads me in the paths of righteousness
For His name's sake.
Yea, though I walk through the valley of
the shadow of death,
I will fear no evil;
For You are with me,
Your rod and Your staff, they comfort me.
You prepare a table before me in the
presence of my enemies;
You anoint my head with oil;
My cup runs over.

Surely goodness and mercy shall follow me
All the days of my life;
And I will dwell in the house of the LORD
Forever. (Psalm 23)

Psalm 23, the most famous of the Psalms is all about relationship. Shepherds and sheep are a common theme throughout Scripture from Genesis to Revelation. The Israelites, as shepherds were despised by the Egyptian aristocracy, but the Israelite shepherds were related to the priesthood, providing animals for sacrifice. King David, before he became king was a shepherd boy and was nearly overlooked when Samuel came to anoint a new king because he was out caring for the sheep. He was known to have killed lions and bears in order to protect the sheep.

The shepherds, watching the flocks at night at the time of the birth of Christ were no doubt, some of those who would have provided animals for sacrifice in the Temple in Jerusalem. Jesus then came as the Good Shepherd, who gave His life for the sheep using shepherds and sheep as themes for parables that He told to explain the heart of the Father for His people. Shepherds in bible times were also very different to shepherds in western countries today. They led the sheep, they protected the sheep and they provided for the sheep. Pastors of churches are sometimes called shepherds, as their role is to guide, guard and feed the sheep.

The Scriptures conclude with the book of Revelation

depicting the Lamb of God seated on the throne receiving worship:

> Saying with a loud voice:
>
> "Worthy is the Lamb who was slain
>
> To receive power and riches and wisdom,
>
> And strength and honor and glory and blessing!" (Revelation 5: 12)

The book which contains the names of those who can enter the New Jerusalem is called the Lambs Book of Life:

> But there shall by no means enter it anything that defiles, or causes an abomination or a lie, but only those who are written in the Lamb's Book of Life. (Revelation21: 27)

David knew about sheep and he also had a relationship with the Lord. In many ways he provided a picture for us of the Shepherd King, Jesus who came later and gave His life for the sheep. Sheep are prone to wander and if you live in a rural area as I do in north Wales it is not uncommon to see sheep on the roads and sometimes trapped in bushes and hedges. The Bible describes this when comparing our behavior to sheep:

All we like sheep have gone astray,

We have turned, every one, to his own way;

And the Lord has laid on Him the iniquity
of us all. (Isaiah 53:6)

David begins the psalm by stating that he has absolute
confidence in the Lord as his shepherd to provide for him.
No luck! David knew that his sheep lacked for nothing
that they needed and similarly he had come to know that
the Lord provided everything for him. We can imagine
David out with his sheep and communing with the Lord
with songs and then we discover in Scripture that he is
described "as a man after God's own heart." He pursued a
close relationship with God and discovered what Jesus said
around a thousand years later to be true:

"But seek first the kingdom of God and
His righteousness, and all these things
shall be added to you. (Matthew 6: 33)

David knew the Lord as his Provider, (YHWH Jireh)
like his forefather Abraham, and then he describes how
the Lord causes him to rest and to know peace as Gideon
had experienced (YHWH Shalom). As he thought about
the Lord who cared and provided for him, he had such a
sense of peace. While he was at rest (YHWH Makadesh)
he could drink cool water, be refreshed and revived. Just as

he provided green pastures and water for the sheep, so he knew that the Lord provided food, drink, restoration and healing for his soul (YHWH Rophe).

Sheep being prone to wander need guidance and so do we! There are right paths and wrong paths! David knew the right paths in which to direct the sheep to keep them from danger and be in a place of security. So it is with the Lord, firstly He makes us righteous (YHWH Tzidkenu), when we rest in the work that Jesus did for us on the cross, pouring out His lifeblood and then He leads us in the right paths that He has ordained for us.

> For He made Him who knew no sin to be sin for us, that we might become he righteousness of God in Him. (2 Corinthians 5: 21)

> And do not present your members as instruments of unrighteousness to sin, but present yourselves to God as being alive from the dead, and your members as instruments of righteousness to God. (Romans 6: 13)

There are many dangers for sheep as there are for the disciple of Jesus. Lions and bears were around at that time and the sheep were no match for them, so the shepherd would rescue them. David had done this at the risk of his own life but he had learned to trust in the Lord and not to fear. John Wesley said not long before he died, "the best of all is that God is with us!" That is a very powerful statement because to know God's presence changes everything. David knew that Presence (YHWH Shammah) in such a real way and that is why he feared so much after he had committed adultery and murder:

> Do not cast me away from Your presence,
>
> And do not take Your Holy Spirit from me. (Psalm 51: 11)

The Israelites camped around the presence of God and Moses had encountered that Presence in Midian when he met with God at the burning bush such that he didn't want to go anywhere without Him. He had learned that without God he couldn't do anything.

> If Your Presence does not go with us, do not bring us up from here. (Exodus 33: 15)

In my own experience, I encountered God as a university student. I often describe it as that which I knew about in my head became real in my life. It was, in reality more than that, for I had experienced the presence of God for myself. I knew that He loved me and I knew that I was His child and that experiential knowledge changed my life forever and strengthened me so I could face all the challenges of life.

David knew the Lord in a very real way and his life was not an easy one. He had a destiny to fulfill and he completed the task that the Lord gave him to do even though he failed at times very seriously.

> "For David, after he had served the purpose of God in his generation, fell asleep, was buried with his fathers and saw corruption. (Acts 13: 36)

David knew God's hand of discipline on his life, but he also knew His authority and saw many wonderful victories (YHWH Nissi) and miracles. The rod is symbolic of correction and the staff of authority.

He had learned to fellowship with the Lord and to experience His presence even when surrounded by enemies and it was that knowledge of the Lord with Him that gave him the strength and sustained him. He experienced the Holy Spirit's anointing in powerful ways and the Lord used him to establish ongoing praise and worship around the tabernacle before the temple was built. Many of the Psalms were written around that period:

> But You are holy,
>
> Enthroned on the praises of Israel. (Psalm 22: 3)

There was a wonderful man of God who lived in north Wales, not so far from us and often when people asked him how he was doing, his reply was, "They're still following me!" The people who asked the question were perplexed, thinking he must have lost his mind! When they enquired further, he explained that it was grace and mercy that were still following him! Although funny, our friend had laid hold of a wonderful truth and it was his experience. He went to be with the Lord some years ago now, but he lived to the age of 103. David knew that blessing in all the challenges of his life with its ups and downs. He knew that he depended on God's grace and needed His mercy.

David has already personalized this psalm but we can make it our own. It's good to say it slowly thinking about each line and how it applies in our daily lives.

YHWH Rohi - I Am the LORD Your Shepherd

The Lord is my shepherd, I shall not want. He makes me to lie down in green pastures; He leads me beside the still waters; He restores my soul; He leads me in the paths of righteousness for His names sake.

Yea, though I walk through the valley of the shadow of death, I will fear no evil, for

You are with me, Your rod and Your staff they comfort me.

You prepare a table before me in the presence of my enemies. You anoint my head with oil. My cup runs over. Surely goodness and mercy shall follow me all the days of my life and I will dwell in the house of the Lord forever.

Today You will guard me, guide me and feed me as I walk with You.

Chapter 10

YHWH TZIDKENU - I AM THE LORD YOUR RIGHTEOUSNESS

"Behold the days are coming", says the
LORD,
"That I will raise to David, a Branch of
righteousness;
A King shall reign and prosper,
And execute judgment and righteousness
in the earth.
In his days Judah will be saved,
And Israel will dwell safely;
Now this is His name by which he will
be called:
THE LORD OUR
RIGHTEOUSNESS." (Jeremiah
23: 5-6)

The subject of righteousness is a key to our relationship with the Lord. The answer to the question which Job asked some thousands of years ago is still just as relevant today:

> How can a man be righteous before God?
> (Job 25: 4)

Jeremiah, who prophesied that the Lord Himself would become His people's righteousness, is a very interesting character in the Bible. His prophetic ministry spanned over a forty year period from 626 to 586 BC, the latter being the year when the temple in Jerusalem was destroyed by the Babylonians. He was a contemporary of Zephaniah, Ezekiel, Habakkuk and Daniel, and he preached at a very critical time in the history of the Jewish people. The ten tribes in the north, known as Israel had been scattered by the Assyrians which left only the two tribes in the south around Jerusalem. Jeremiah saw many kings of Judah come and go during his lifetime.

He was born during the reign of Manasseh, one of the most wicked kings that Judah had. It was during his reign that, according to Jewish tradition, Isaiah the prophet was sawn in two inside a hollow tree! His crime was prophesying the word of God. Jeremiah was born at Anathoth which was very close to Jerusalem and was appointed to be a prophet before he was born. This was a daunting call for him and he didn't feel adequate for the job:

Then the word of the Lord came to me saying:

> "Before I formed you in the womb I knew you;
>
> Before you were born I sanctified you;
>
> I ordained you as a prophet to the nations."
>
> Then said I, "Ah, Lord God!
>
> Behold, I cannot speak, for I am a youth."
> (Jeremiah 1: 4-6)

Jeremiah's message was similar to other prophets such as Ezekiel, because he observed the backsliding of a nation. The main issues were idolatry, immorality and injustice. Jerusalem was no longer a safe place, so children couldn't play in the streets and older people were afraid to leave their homes. Child sacrifice was being practiced and idols were brought into the temple in direct disobedience to the commandments which the Lord had given through Moses.

It was into this situation that Jeremiah was called to prophesy, and he particularly aimed his message at the leaders, the false prophets, the priests, and the kings who had to take a major part of the responsibility for the situation. The false prophets contradicted Jeremiah's message and they told the people what they wanted to hear, the priests had allowed idol worship in the temple and the kings had failed to uphold God's laws. The blessings of God promised to the Jewish people in the Mosaic covenant were conditional upon their obedience. Jeremiah knew this and he warned of impending disaster.

Jeremiah's prophecies came to pass! One of them related to a man called Hananiah, who was a false prophet and had been telling the people that their enemies would be destroyed and they had nothing to worry about. Jeremiah told the people not to trust in such lies and that Hananiah would die that same year because of is rebellion. Two months later Hananiah died, just as Jeremiah had prophesied. He prophesied that the danger this time would not come from Assyria but from Babylon whose armies would invade from the north.

It wasn't all bad news, however because Jeremiah prophesied, along with other biblical prophets, that there was hope. He prophesied that the exile would be limited to seventy years after which there would be some restoration. Daniel the prophet, a contemporary of Jeremiah read this prophecy when in Babylon and he must have been greatly encouraged by it and so prayed:

> In the first year of his reign I, Daniel, understood by the books the number of the years specified by the word of the LORD through Jeremiah the prophet, that He would accomplish seventy years in the desolations of Jerusalem.

Then I set my face toward the Lord God to make request by prayer and supplications, with fasting, sackcloth, and ashes. (Daniel 9: 2-3)

Daniel had understood that they didn't deserve anything from God, because of their disobedience but he knew that God is good and relied on His mercy:

"To the Lord our God belong mercy and forgiveness, though we have rebelled against Him. (Daniel 9:9)

Jeremiah also prophesied that a day would come when God would make a new covenant with His people. The Mosaic covenant was conditional upon the obedience of God's people and this was the problem. They were just incapable of keeping the laws! This is also our problem and it is the problem of the human race. We are incapable of changing our hearts no matter how many laws or rules we make. Jeremiah gave hope, not only of restoration to the land for the Jews but also for a change in the covenant:

"Behold the days are coming, says the LORD, when I will make a new covenant with the house of Israel and with the house of Judah –

"not according to the covenant that I made with their fathers in the day that I took them by the hand to lead them out of the land of Egypt, My covenant which they broke, though I was a husband to them, says the LORD.

"But this is the covenant that I will make with the house of Israel after those days, says the LORD: I will put My law in their minds, and write it on their hearts, and I will be their God and they shall be My people. (Jeremiah 31: 31-33)

This new covenant which Jeremiah is prophesying about is contrasted with the covenant God made with the Israelites through Moses in Sinai after they had been delivered from slavery in Egypt. This is often known as the Mosaic covenant because Moses was God's instrument at the time. This covenant according to the letter to the Hebrews is now obsolete:

In that He says, "A new covenant," He has made the first obsolete. Now what is becoming obsolete and growing old is ready to vanish away. (Hebrews 8: 13)

The Mosaic covenant promised blessings, but only if the laws were obeyed and Paul explains that if righteousness is to be obtained by the Mosaic covenant then the whole law has to be kept, otherwise instead of blessings curses will follow:

> For as many are of the works of the law are under a curse; for it is written, "Cursed is everyone who does not continue in all things which are written in the book of the law, to do them." (Galatians 3: 10)

The Mosaic covenant therefore brings with it a curse because of the inability of God's people to keep it. The purpose of the Mosaic covenant is to show us our utter depravity and inability to keep God's laws in our own strength. Isn't this our experience? The harder we try in own strength to overcome a particular bad habit or character trait, often the worse we become! So the Mosaic laws are to act as a means of revealing to us our need of a Savior!

> Therefore the law was our tutor to bring us to Christ, that we might be justified by faith. (Galatians 3: 24)

The good news is that Jesus Christ fulfilled all the requirements of the Mosaic Law. He lived under the Law and He came to fulfill it:

> "Do not think I came to destroy the Law
> or the Prophets. I did not come to destroy
> but to fulfill. (Matthew 5: 17)

This is good news for those who know that they have not kept God's laws or lived up to His requirements. Jesus did it all on our behalf! He paid a debt He didn't owe and He lived a life that we couldn't live. He did it because He loves us!

The new covenant deals with the root of the problem which is the human heart. There is an inner change the life of Christ comes to live inside us when we confess Jesus as our Lord and receive the Holy Spirit. We then have a new power and a new strength that we didn't have before! God's laws are written on our hearts. Christ lives in us by the Holy Spirit and the apostolic letters of the New Testament describe what is available to us in Christ. We have His love, His righteousness, His power and His holiness. This is all available to us in Christ, who has taken up residence in us by the Holy Spirit. A great exchange has taken place! My sin was taken on the cross and He gave me His righteousness when I received Him. We have a righteousness which has been given to us by faith and which we haven't earned or deserved! This is known as God's grace.

But now the righteousness of God apart from the law is revealed, being witnessed by the Law and the Prophets,

even the righteousness of God, through faith in Jesus Christ, to all and on all who believe. For there is no difference;

for all have sinned and fall short of the glory of God,

being justified freely by His grace through the redemption that is in Christ Jesus. (Romans 3: 21-24)

How does the righteousness that has been given to us by faith and is in Christ who lives in us, manifest in our experience? The answer is by being filled with the Holy Spirit and renewing our minds.

I beseech you therefore, brethren, by the mercies of God, that you present your bodies a living sacrifice, holy, acceptable to God, which is your reasonable service.

And do not be conformed to this world, but be transformed by the renewing of your mind, that you may prove what is

> that good and acceptable and perfect will
> of God. (Romans 12: 1-2)

What an amazing gospel we have to proclaim! I often think when in Nepal or India and see hundreds of believers worshipping the Lord and not many years previously, many of them were far from God, worshipping idols. The Mosaic covenant brought with it blessings and curses. Blessings for obedience and curses for disobedience. The curses included abject poverty, mental illness, various diseases as well as other things and it is very interesting to see how prevalent these curses are in countries like Nepal and India where there is much idol worship. It has been so encouraging to see thousands of Nepalese respond to the gospel in Nepal at our meetings and as they receive Christ and are discipled in the faith so the curse is broken over their lives.

The moment we receive Christ, God counts us as righteous. We should no longer view ourselves as sinners or live under condemnation (even though we still have struggles and can still sin). If we sin we confess and repent, then move on knowing that we are not only forgiven but have been made righteous. Justified as someone explained it is just..as..if..I'd never sinned. We can renew our minds to who we are in Christ and then we will be transformed so that what we have in Christ in our spirit will be released into or experience. This involves the mind and the body.

It is well worth noting, that the prophecy given to God's people about righteousness, was given when they were in one of their most wayward states. This reminds us not only that God's love and promises for the restoration of Israel are still valid, but also that the gospel is the only true hope for all those who are estranged from Him. His heart of love wants all to come to Him to find real life.

> "For we will surely die and become like spilled water on the ground, which cannot be gathered up again. Yet God does not take away life, but He devises means, so that his banished ones are not expelled from Him. (2 Samuel 14: 14)

> The Lord is not slack concerning His promise, as some count slackness, but is longsuffering toward us, not willing that any should perish but that all should come to repentance. (2 Peter 3: 9)

This confession is based on 2 Corinthians 5: 21 and Romans 8: 1 and it helps us to renew our minds to the truth that God has imputed to us the righteousness of Jesus Christ. This is something that God has done for us because of the work of Jesus Christ on the cross. It is not something that we have earned or deserved.

> YHWH Tzidkenu - I Am the LORD
> Your Righteousness

There is therefore now no condemnation for me, because I am in Christ Jesus. For the law of the Spirit of life in Christ has made me free from the law of sin and death.

I am free from sin's guilt condemnation and shame because Jesus took it all for me at the cross.

He (Jesus), who knew no sin, was made to be sin for me, so that I might become the righteousness of God in Christ.

By God's grace I am the righteousness of God in Christ.

I am the righteousness of God in Christ

Chapter 11

YHWH SHAMMAH - I AM THE LORD WHO IS THERE

"All the way around shall be eighteen thousand cubits; and the name of the city from that day shall be: THE LORD IS THERE." (Ezekiel 48: 35)

The awareness of the presence of God changes everything! I remember walking through the streets of Kathmandu on mission with my team when there were tanks lining the streets and the Nepalese army soldiers were standing guard at strategic points. As we were officially classed as tourists, we were allowed to walk in the streets but there was a curfew for the local residents. The Maoist soldiers had mustered an army together, and had managed to control certain areas and were now marching towards Kathmandu.

We had been able to conduct some meetings on the outskirts of the city and the hosting pastor, our good friend Min Raj Dulal, was accompanying us to the point where the curfew for him started. After this, we were on our own and had to walk about 2 or 3 miles to the Hotel where we were staying. The streets were deserted which was very unusual, as normally they were full of traffic with motorbikes and other vehicles appearing to travel in all directions and the sound of horns would be incessant.

This day, however, was different; there was an eerie silence and soldiers eying us suspiciously with their guns at the ready. Strangely, I felt no fear and experienced what the Bible calls, "the peace of God that passes understanding." It's a peace that transcends our natural thinking. It was God's manifest presence and I knew that people were praying back home. It is often said, that the safest place for us to be is in the will of God and it is true. We have the promise of God's presence and the angels around us. I don't have all the answers as to why some are martyred and others are spared. I do know, however, that God is faithful to His word and those who are martyred for Christ go on to a great reward in His continual presence.

We have looked at the earlier life of Ezekiel when considering "YHWH Makadesh, I Am the LORD Your Sanctifier," but now we need to consider his later years of ministry to set the context for "YHWH Shammah, I Am the LORD Who Is There." The later years of Ezekiel's ministry relate to the restoration of Israel and the temple in Jerusalem. Much of these later prophecies in Ezekiel's are yet to be fulfilled. Taking the Bible as a whole, over eighty per cent of the prophecies have already been fulfilled so we can be very confident that the remaining twenty per cent will also be fulfilled!

Ezekiel was about fifty years of age when making these prophecies and they followed a period of silence when God did not release him to speak:

> "I will make your tongue cling to the roof
> of your mouth, so that you shall be mute
> and not be one to rebuke them, though
> they are a rebellious house.
>
> "But when I speak with you, I will open
> your mouth, and you shall say to them....
> (Ezekiel 3: 26-27)
>
> 'And you, son of man – will it not be in
> the day when I take from them their
> stronghold, their joy and their glory, the
> desire of their eyes, and that on which they
> set their minds, their sons and daughters:
>
> 'on that day one who escapes will come to
> you to let you hear it with your ears;
>
> 'on that day your mouth will be opened to
> him who has escaped; you shall speak and

> no longer be mute. Thus you will be a sign
> to them, and they shall know that I am the
> LORD.'" (Ezekiel 24: 25-27)

From now onwards in the book of Ezekiel, the message is about restoration. Ezekiel's wife had died at the same time that the temple in Jerusalem was destroyed and this was as a prophetic sign that as Ezekiel was grieving over the wife that he loved so the Lord grieved over the city and the people that He loved.

This is not the end, there is hope and these prophecies of restoration are full of hope for Israel. We too, can learn from this about God's character that even when there is failure, waywardness and a turning away from God's purposes, whether it is an individual, a church or a nation there is hope because God's heart is to restore.

The loss of the temple for God's people was devastating. The temple in those days was the place where His presence was, so to lose the temple was for the glory of God to depart and this is exactly as Ezekiel had seen it in visions years before it happened:

> Then the glory of the Lord departed from
> the threshold of the temple and stood over
> the cherubim. (Ezekiel 10: 18)

Ezekiel prophesies not only the restoration of the Jewish people to the land, but also the restoration of the temple and the glory of God. These prophecies in the latter part of Ezekiel's ministry were given in the twenty-fifth year of his exile when he was fifty. The restoration of the Jews to the land of Israel clearly has a meaning beyond the return after the seventy years which Jeremiah prophesied about. After this exile in Babylon, the Jews returned only from Babylon but Ezekiel is now prophesying about a future date because he speaks about returning from among all the countries where they have been scattered:

> "For I will take you from among the nations, gather you out of all countries and bring you into your own land.

> "Then I will sprinkle clean water on you, and you shall be clean. I will cleanse you from all your filthiness and from all your idols.

> "I will give you a new heart and put a new spirit within you; I will take the heart of stone out of your flesh and give you a heart of flesh.

> "I will put My Spirit within you and cause you to walk in My statutes, and you will keep My judgments and do them. (Ezekiel 36: 24-26)

It is important to notice the order of this restoration, first is the return of the Jewish people to the land, and then they are washed, cleansed and receive the Holy Spirit. This is so much like Jeremiah's prophecy of the new covenant which we discussed when considering "YHWH Tzidkenu, I Am the LORD Your Righteousness."

. Another aspect of these prophecies is that the twelve tribes of Israel will be united again. The kingdom of Israel was divided after Solomon's reign into the northern kingdom, Israel, represented by Ephraim, the name for the ten tribes and Judah representing the southern kingdom being the larger of the two remaining tribes. Today Jewish people from all twelve tribes have returned and are returning to the land as one nation:

> "say to them, 'Thus says the LORD GOD: "Surely I will take the stick of Joseph, which is in the hand of Ephraim, and the tribes of Israel, his companions and I will join them with it, with the stick of Judah and make them one one stick and they will be one in My hand."' (Ezekiel 37: 19)

The prophecy states that this is done for a testimony to the nations around:

> "Then the nations which are left all around you shall know that I, the LORD have

> rebuilt the ruined places and planted what
> was desolate. I, the LORD have spoken it,
> and I will do it. (Ezekiel 36: 36)

The return of the Jewish people to the land of Israel, to be re-born as a nation with the revived Hebrew language against so much opposition is miraculous and a fulfillment of biblical prophecy. It is a testimony to the truth of God's word and His faithfulness.

The temple will also be restored and the glory of God will return:

> The Spirit lifted me up and brought me
> into the inner court; and behold, the glory
> of the LORD filled the temple. (Ezekiel
> 43: 5)

This is for a future date, probably during the thousand reign of Christ and relates to Israel.

At this present time according to the New Testament, we are God's temple who have the Holy Spirit living in us. We can be confident that God who keeps His covenant with Israel, keeps His covenant with us because we have been brought into this new covenant by the blood of Jesus. As His people we have the promise of His abiding presence. He dwells in us and when we gather together as believers He promises to be there in a special way:

> For where two or three are gathered
> together in My name, I am there in the
> midst of them. (Matthew 18: 20)

In our church in Beaumaris, Anglesey we have been very blessed to have folk on holiday to visit. Some of them have testified how they have experienced God's presence in the services and that their lives have been impacted by the Lord. In God's presence our hearts are lifted, we are encouraged, sometimes people are healed, others are convicted but it should all be good and edifying.

Paul describes this outcome of a Holy Spirit filled gathering where the gifts of the Spirit are functioning:

> But if all prophesy, and an unbeliever or
> an uninformed person comes in, he is
> convinced by all, he is convicted by all.
>
> And thus the secrets of his heart are
> revealed; and so, falling down on his face,
> he will worship God and report that God
> is truly among you. (1 Corinthians 14:
> 24-25)

Some people have lived in such a close relationship with the Lord that they significantly affect the people that they come into contact with the manifest presence of God. There are many stories about men of God like John Wesley, who when a crowd of people discovered where he was staying decided to go to the house to kill him. They banged on the door and the housekeeper did not know what to do, but John Wesley told her to open the door. As he came down the staircase he just looked at them and they found that they could not do anything except walk away!

Moses so valued and depended on God's presence that he didn't want to go anywhere unless he knew that the Lord was going with him:

> Then he said to Him, "If Your Presence does not go with us, do not bring us up from here. (Exodus 33: 15)

There is a well known story told about the English preacher Smith Wigglesworth, when once he was on a train and as he was there seated, without having spoken a word another man in the carriage looked at him and said, "Sir, you convict me of my sin!" That is God's presence!

We can cultivate an awareness of God's presence by spending time with Him, meditating on scripture, feeding on good sound teaching that builds faith. Also spending time in worship and waiting on God, listening to Him speak to our hearts very often through scripture. Brother Lawrence learned to abide in that Presence even when carrying out very mundane duties. His intimate relationship with God was recorded in a book which was compiled after his death in 1691 entitled, "The practice of the Presence of God." This has subsequently become a

Christian classic. What an awesome privilege to have the Lord with us! John Wesley said not long before he passed into eternity, "The best of all is that God is with us!"

Through all the changing scenes of life, the knowledge of His abiding presence changes everything. A small child can go to many places if he has his Dad (or Mum) with him, whereas on his own he would be afraid. We are never alone because, as He demonstrated to His ancient people," YHWH Shammah, I Am There!"

This confession is based on Deuteronomy 31: 8, Joshua 1: 9, Matthew 28: 20 and Hebrews 13: 5 – 6.

> YHWH Shammah - I Am the LORD Who Is There
>
> The Lord is with me today. He has said, "I will never leave you or forsake you," so that I can boldly say, "The Lord is my helper, therefore, I will not fear, what can man do to me."

APPENDIX 1: HOW TO HAVE A RELATIONSHIP WITH GOD

The whole subject of confessing the word of God will not mean much to anyone who doesn't have a relationship with God through faith in Jesus Christ. If you are not sure about this, there is no better time to make sure than now and the following explains how you can!

The fundamental problem of the human race is alienation from God due to Adam and Eve's disobedience. God is holy and we are not but He has provided a solution. Only Jesus Christ was able to live in perfect obedience to His Father all of His life. As God's only begotten Son He became the perfect sinless sacrifice to die the death and take the punishment that we deserved on the cross. His blood was accepted by the Father, as it represented the poured out life of the sinless Saviour. He rose again from the dead and all who repent and receive Jesus Christ as Lord and Saviour can also receive forgiveness, cleansing and come into a wonderful relationship with God the Father that is eternal. The Bible describes this as being saved.

What a wonderful blessing it is to know complete forgiveness! We don't have to live in guilt and condemnation for past sin and failure but we can know total acceptance and forgiveness through Jesus work on the cross for us! We don't have to fear going to Hell when we die but can be assured of being with the Lord in Heaven, not because we have earned or deserved it but because it is God's free gift to all who call upon the Lord Jesus. However we don't have to wait until we go to Heaven before we can experience this relationship because it starts as soon as we turn to Him

You can received Christ by praying the prayer written out below could help you or you could pray something similar along these lines in your own words:

> Father God, I come to You in the name of Jesus. I believe that Jesus Christ died on the cross taking the punishment for my sin. I repent and give my life to You. forgive me and cleanse my by the precious blood of Jesus. I confess Jesus as Lord of my life and I ask You to fill me with Your Holy Spirit.

If you prayed that sincerely, God heard and answered your prayer!

> If we confess our sins, He is faithful and
> just to forgive us our sins and to cleanse
> us from all unrighteousness. (1John 1: 9)

> that if you confess with your mouth the
> Lord Jesus and believe in your heart that
> God has raised Him from the dead, you
> will be saved. (Romans 10: 9)

Now that you have received Christ and know that
you are forgiven you will want to obey Him. The first
step of obedience is to be baptized in water. Baptism in
water signifies your identification with the death and
resurrection of Jesus. Your old life has died and our new
life has begun! You are now, in Christ, and are not the
same anymore. The Lord wants you to see yourself as He
sees you and this involves a new confession, that is a new
way of speaking.

After baptism in water you will need to be filled or
baptized with the Holy Spirit. This will enable you to
experience the power of the Holy Spirit in your lives.

> Then Peter said to them, "Repent, and let
> everyone of you be baptized in the name
> of Jesus Christ for the remission of sins;
> and you shall receive the gift of the Holy
> Spirit. (Acts 2: 38)

How can you receive this? You come to the Lord

having received cleansing by the blood of Jesus from all sin and then by faith receive the infilling of the Holy Spirit. It's as easy as breathing in the air! Open your heart to Him and as words rise up from your inner being (not your own language), speak them out in faith. There will be a release of God's power as you do this and you will experience God's peace and presence. He will give you a strength and a power that you didn't have before so that you can overcome temptation.

This experience changed my life and countless others. I was speaking to a pastor friend few years ago, who lives in quite a remote part of India. Although he was brought up in church, he had never been taught about the baptism in the Holy Spirit. I explained some things to him and he asked if he could come to some meetings that we were holding in Nepal so that I could pray for him. I told him that he didn't need to wait until then but that I would pray for him over the phone. I prayed and he received the gift of tongues. A few days later he contacted me and testified that he had prayed for some others to receive the baptism in the Holy Spirit. They also received, demons came out of people and some amazing miracle healings took place! To God be the glory! It doesn't have to be complicated or take a long time!

The gift of tongues is a prayer language that the Holy Spirit gives us and by using it God's power is released into our lives in a wonderful way. The other gifts of the Holy Spirit in accordance with 1 Corinthians 12 also become available to us. If you are a new believer, it is important that you become part of a Bible believing church fellowship so that you can grow in your Christian life using these gifts as taught in the New Testament.

> While Peter was still speaking these words, the Holy Spirit fell upon all those who heard the word.
>
> And those of the circumcision who believed were astonished, as many as came with Peter, because the gift of the Holy Spirit had been poured out on the Gentiles also.
>
> For they heard them speak with tongues and magnify God. (Acts 10: 44-46)
>
> "And as I began to speak, the Holy Spirit fell upon them, as upon us at the beginning.
>
> Then I remembered the word of the Lord, how He said, 'John indeed baptized with water, but you shall be baptized with the Holy Spirit.'
>
> If therefore God gave them the same gift as He gave us when we believed on the

Lord Jesus Christ, who was I that I could withstand God?" (Acts 11: 15 – 17)

"Therefore I say to you, whatever things you ask when you pray, believe that you receive them, and you will have them. (Mark 11: 24)

"If you then, being evil, know how to give good gifts to your children, how much more will your heavenly Father give the Holy Spirit to those who ask Him!" (Luke 11: 13)

You can be confident that when you have prayed sincerely the Lord has heard you and you can then thank and praise Him.

APPENDIX 2: DAILY CONFESSIONS BASED ON EIGHT REVELATIONS OF GOD'S CHARACTER

1. YHWH Jireh - I Am the LORD Your Provovider

    The Lord is my Provider

    And my God shall supply all my need according to His riches in glory by Christ Jesus.

    I am blessed with every spiritual blessing in heavenly places in Christ.

    The blessing of the Lord makes me rich and He adds no sorrow with it.

    I declare today that I am blessed spiritually, intellectually, emotionally, physically, my family is blessed, my work is blessed, my ministry is blessed and my finances are blessed.

2. YHWH Rophe - I Am the LORD Your Healer

The Lord is my healer.

The chastisement for our peace was upon Him and by His stripes we are healed.

The chastisement for my peace was upon Him and by His stripes I am healed.

By his stripes I was healed.

Since by His stripes I was healed then by His stripes I am healed.

Since by His stripes I am healed then I am healed!

He sent forth His word and He healed them.

He sent forth His word and He healed me.

Since He sent forth His word and healed me then I am healed!

Bless the Lord O my soul and all that is within me bless His holy name.

He has forgiven all your sins and He has healed all your diseases.

He has forgiven all my sins and He has healed all my diseases.

Since He has healed all my diseases then I am healed!

3. YHWH Nissi - I Am the LORD Your Banner

The Lord is my banner, the One who gives me victory.

I have total victory in Christ.

The Lord gives me victory everywhere I go.

I am more than a conqueror through Christ who strengthens me.

4. YHWH Shalom - I Am the LORD Your peace

The Lord is my peace.

I will in nothing be anxious, but I will in everything by prayer with supplication and thanksgiving let my requests be made known unto God and the peace of God which surpasses all understanding will guard my heart and mind through Christ Jesus.

5. YHWH Makadesh - I Am the LORD who Sanctifies You

The Lord is my sanctifier.

And now the God of peace will sanctify me completely, my whole, spirit, soul and body.

For me to live is Christ.

Christ lives in me.

Father God, today I receive from You all that I need to live for You. Forgiveness and cleansing by the blood of Jesus and a fresh infilling of the Holy Spirit to captivate my heart. Let Your refining fire go though my heart, burn out anything that doesn't please You, set my heart ablaze with love and passion for You. I offer to You my spirit, soul and body to be set apart for You. For Your glory. Amen.

6. YHWH Rohi - I Am the LORD Your Shepherd

The Lord is my shepherd, I shall not want. He makes me to lie down in green pastures; He leads me beside the still waters; He restores my soul; He leads me in the paths of righteousness for His names sake.

Yea, though I walk through the valley of the shadow of death, I will fear no evil, for You are with me, Your rod and Your staff they comfort me.

You prepare a table before me in the presence of my enemies. You anoint my head with oil. My cup runs over. Surely goodness and mercy shall follow me all the days of my life and I will dwell in the house of the Lord forever.

Today You will guard me, guide me and feed me as I walk with You.

7. YHWH Tzidkenu - I Am the LORD Your Righteousness

There is therefore now no condemnation for me because I am in Christ Jesus. For the law of the Spirit of life in Christ has made me free from the law of sin and death.

I am free from sin's guilt condemnation and shame because Jesus took it all away for me at the cross.

He made Him (Jesus), who knew no sin to be sin for me so that I might become the righteousness of God in Christ.

By God's grace I am the righteousness of God in Christ.

I am the righteousness of God in Christ.

8. YHWH Shammah - I Am the LORD who Is There

The Lord is with me today. He has said, "I will never leave you or forsake you," so that I can boldly say, "The Lord is my helper, therefore, I will not fear, what can man do to me."

ABOUT THE AUTHOR

Philip Evans is a graduate of the University of Manchester where he studied civil engineering. After graduating from university he worked with Operation Mobilization in Spain and  Israel. Philip also has an M.A. from ForMission College of Theology and York St. John University. Together with his wife Margaret they have led the work at Oasis Church, Anglesey since 1992 and have ministered in the USA, Europe, Africa and Asia. Over the years they have been privileged to see thousands come to Christ, healing miracles and believers experiencing the power of the Holy Spirit. They have also helped with the training of leaders and church planting in Nepal. Margaret has taught the Bible Explorer program to hundreds of school children throughout Anglesey, has led many school assemblies in local schools and is a popular speaker at "Women's Aglow" meetings.

Printed in the United States
By Bookmasters